T.

This ... ascinating story of Mildred Cable's adventures across the Gobi Desert, in the company of Evangeline and Francesca French.

As a pioneer missionary and traveller for Christ, Mildred Cable has a memorable place in the Christian story, and this account of where she went and what she did will interest and thrill readers of all ages.

Stories of Faith and Fame

edited by Cecil Northcott

STAR OVER GOBI

ALL ABOARD FOR THE GOBI

STAR OVER GOBI

The Story of Mildred Cable

by
CECIL NORTHCOTT

LUTTERWORTH PRESS
LONDON

MADE AND PRINTED IN GREAT BRITAIN BY
EBENEZER BAYLIS AND SON, LIMITED, THE
TRINITY PRESS, WORCESTER, AND LONDON

CONTENTS

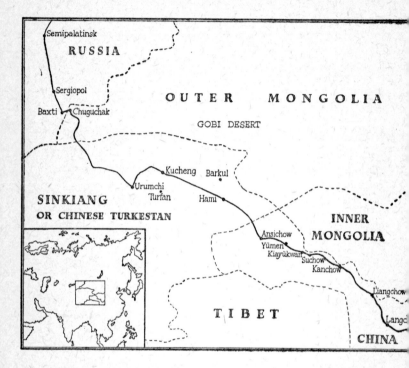

The thick line shows the route of Mildred Cable's travels across the Gobi Desert. The inset map shows the same area on a map of Asia

1

DREAMS COME TRUE

"I THINK the Lord wants you in China," said the speaker as she walked from the meeting with Mildred Cable. The teen-age girl in the summer of 1893, just fourteen years old, was already thinking seriously of going overseas to serve God. She had listened eagerly to the missionary home from China. There was something about her which both attracted and repelled Mildred Cable. Her dress was very plain, so plain that the inscription woven into the collar of her dress stood out in striking prominence, "Jesus He shall save."

Mildred looked up at the speaker as they walked away from the meeting and asked, "Do all missionaries wear texts like that?"

"No," replied her friend, "but in China I always do and I see no reason for dropping it here."

"If I went to be a missionary," said Mildred, "I would go to India."

"You must go where the Lord sends you, my dear. If you are Christ's you must be His entirely."

That conversation made a deep impression on the youthful Mildred Cable. But she wondered whether all missionaries were like that with texts on their collars, and so sure of what God wanted them to do. She decided to find out more about the China Inland Mission which sent people like that to China.

The opportunity came one day to visit the Candidates Department of the mission in North London, which she found a busy and happy place full of eager, dedicated people with one chief object in view: to tell the people of China about Christ. It was that simple, clear purpose that won the heart of Mildred Cable as she learned more about the mission and its purpose. Her understanding deepened when, on leaving school, she spent six months in the mission's training home to see whether her calling to be a missionary was a permanent one or just a passing phase in the life of an intense, impressionable adolescent girl.

At the end of that time there was no doubt in Mildred's heart where her calling in life lay, and her family gradually came to accept the fact that Mildred was to be a missionary. So with the enthusiasm of one who knows what she wants to do Mildred Cable set herself to prepare for China. There was no time to lose to serve Him with her whole life. It was suggested that she might take a full medical course and become a fully qualified doctor, but that would have taken up too many years in preparation. She wanted her dream to come true quickly.

So a special plan was arranged with the help of a pioneer woman scientist in London whereby Mildred followed a course of study in medicine. This would help her to serve the people of China as fully as possible in His name. So from Monday to Saturday Mildred attended lectures and classes, and eventually went to live with her clever scientific friend, who saw the purpose in Mildred's heart and was ready to help her fulfil it.

*   *   *

But something else happened too which deepened the purpose. In North London at Tollington Park a tall young preacher with a mop of black hair was drawing crowded congregations to the Congregational Church. It was Campbell Morgan, then at the beginning of a ministry destined to be a great blessing to many both in Britain and America. Mildred was fascinated by the way he used the Bible. He inspired his audiences to search the Scriptures, to study them, and find out how God worked. He opened the Bible for Mildred in a new way and all during her life the Book of Books was always providing her with new treasures.

It was not enough, however, to study the Bible

and keep its rich fruits for oneself. Mildred, like scores of other young people, under Campbell Morgan's ministry was expected to tell others about Jesus. So she joined the evangelistic band which on Sunday evenings conducted services in the Variety Hall not far from the church. There in an atmosphere of singing, music, and humour the gospel was preached and many were led to give their lives to Christ.

Step by step Mildred Cable's life was prepared for China. The slim, middle-height young woman with the quick glance and brisk ways saw her dream gradually shaping. Would it really come true?

Suddenly the news from China was bad. The newspapers were full of stories of the most horrible atrocities in China. In hatred of "the foreigners" the Boxer Rising had resulted in the killing of many missionaries. In the lonely places of inland China many brave spirits had bowed their heads to the sword. It looked as if missions for many years to come would not be able to start work again, and the set-back would be permanent.

Mildred's heart was heavy. Her road seemed blocked. Her natural, youthful zeal to do things, and her decision to give her life for Christ, were being thwarted. At this time, too, her own personal life suffered a big disappointment, and the one with whom she shared her deepest thoughts about her missionary calling turned away from the vision. Mildred knew the sorrows of loneliness, and the sadness of dreams not coming true.

*　　*　　*

But as the cloud came down suddenly so it lifted. The way to China opened up and on September 25, 1901, in her twenty-second year, Mildred Cable sailed for China, her father going with her as far as the United States. Her first year in China was spent in language study. Mildred bent her energies to a mastery of the intricate Chinese tongue which stood her in good stead years later when she took the road across the Gobi Desert. Then the great decision of her place of work was made. She was to go to Hwochow in the far distant province of Shansi, where work was just beginning again after the Boxer Rising.

The young recruit was to travel with a more senior missionary—Evangeline French, who looked at her frail companion and wondered how she would stand up to the long days of jolting in a Chinese cart. For over a week along the "Big Road" to the north-west from Taiyuanfu the two missionaries jogged in the cart. In the heat and dust the carter slowly drove his mules through the narrow gullies and across the bare open plain. Mildred's keen eyes took in everything, and she began to learn that time and patience in China settle every problem in the end. Whenever two carts met on the narrow road there was bound to be trouble in passing. She wrote home to her friends:

> After endless discussion, amid comforting whiffs of tobacco he proceeds to think of a plan whereby the deadlock may be overcome. How they manage to extricate themselves, no one ever knows. Some of the bank comes down, yells and shouts do their part, and at last the traffic which may now amount to fifty waiting carts, slowly passes by.

It was her first long introduction to cart travel, a preparation for the long years of her Gobi Desert journeys, and by her side was the first of her devoted companions—Eva French—who was to share her life.

At Hwochow the house they were to occupy was not ready, so the two friends set off on a country journey to see the village people they were to live amongst. Mildred tied up her belongings in big square handkerchiefs, threw her wadded quilt in its large bed-bag over the donkey and was hoisted on to the donkey's back. They wandered leisurely from village to village enjoying the bright sunshine, waving to the children and the women who cried, "Come again, come again, come again soon."

Down past the great tanks of lotus flowers, across the shallow river where the donkey-man stripped off his shoes and socks to lead her donkey across the stream, and on to the home of Giang, the church elder who had once been an opium smoker and gambler. Mildred revelled in it all, especially in the cave which Giang set aside for their temporary home. This is really China, she thought. This is home.

*   *   *

Back in Hwochow Mildred met the little church of some thirty people, the company gathered over the years after much faithful work. It seemed so tiny and feeble, and she soon discovered that it was torn internally by jealousies and hatreds. There was Mr. Lan who loved money and was always in debt; Mr. Diao, a poor specimen of a man and none had confidence in him; Mr. Tu who "trusted God" and yet who seemed so weak. Most of them had been brought to Christ through the faithful preaching and life of Pastor Hsi, but they were all so old and lacked leadership.

Mildred Cable and Evangeline French were faced with a big decision. How could they train new leaders for the church? How could they influence the women and the children? They both loved the free life of the travelling missionary wandering through the villages, distributing the Scriptures, talking to the people in their homes; but they both knew that Hwochow needed years of intensive, patient work to reap a harvest.

So in the small inner courtyard of the Hwochow house two rooms were set aside for a girls' school. Those two rooms were soon crowded with pupils. In addition, married women were welcome for thirty days at a time to receive Christian instruction. The Hwochow Christian community began to throb with new life under the motto, "When the pressure of the work is too heavy, then extend the work."

Round many of the villages in the Hwochow area grew the poppies loved by the opium smokers, and in every village there were opium addicts who loved the opium pipe and the whiff of smoke which gave them false dreams of happiness. For them the Hwochow Christians prepared an opium refuge where kindness and treatment with what the people called "the pill of life", "the pill of strength" and "the pill of restoration" brought many cures from opium smoking.

*   *   *

Service, teaching, visiting, endless conversations, and village visiting filled in the busy years of Mildred Cable's first period in China. Home in Britain in 1908 she spoke about her dream of a larger Women's Bible School, and Dr. Campbell Morgan's congregation at Westminster Chapel helped to complete the £500 needed for that venture.

Mildred's medical training was a splendid asset to her in the town and in the schools. Sometimes the Mandarin of Hwochow asked her to come and cure the toothache of his ladies, which she did by carefully secreting the forceps under her Chinese dress and bringing them swiftly to work while the lady was laughing with her mouth open. Teeth extraction was a popular occasion because the tooth was always carefully preserved as a family heirloom.

Mildred's intense love of individual people and her care for them came out in her friendship with many of the girls who came to the school. One of them was "Flower of Love", who became a pupil in the school at the age of twelve and attended regularly until she was eighteen. "Bright, happy and full of girlish enthusiasm she yielded her heart to Christ," wrote Mildred Cable, "and with her girl companions rejoiced in her new-found joy. A horror of great darkness fell upon her soul when the news was broken to her that her parents had contracted for her a marriage with a heathen man, and yielding to uncontrollable grief she became seriously ill."

"Flower of Love" asked for the prayers of all in the mission that the engagement would be broken off and Mildred had the joy of telling "Flower of Love" the good news that prayer had been answered. "Flower of Love's" response was to give her whole life to the service of God.

Months passed and the parents secretly prepared another marriage with "a man whose wealth was accumulated by wrong-doing, and before any step could be taken Flower of Love was his bride. For months she struggled alone in the city to which she had been taken, and then his orders were given that intercourse with foreigners must cease. The fight was too hard, and weary she yielded and allowed herself to drift with the tide."

It was heart-breaking for Mildred Cable to see a favourite pupil on whom she had lavished so much care slip away into a sinful life. "She is beyond my reach," she wrote, "but her broken heart will yet, I believe, find a resting place upon her Saviour's breast."

*   *   *

One of the excitements of Mildred's years at Hwochow was the six days' special mission to the women of the church and district. On donkey back, in mule carts and on foot the women came in from the villages. Over three hundred women packed the little church.

"Large numbers of heathen," wrote Mildred Cable to her friends, "attracted by the unique sight of so large a concourse of women swelled the numbers at the daily evangelistic meetings, and it was an inspiration to see the new church packed with women and girls listening to the gospel message. A room was set apart where silence was observed, that those who wished to do so might pray without fear of disturbance. A band of helpers was appointed to teach the passage for the day, and outside the church in an adjoining court was a book-stall and here a brisk trade was done in hymn-sheets, gospels and block-printed texts."

It was a strenuous occasion, for, like all things Mildred Cable had a hand in, it was well organized and thoroughly done. The men of the church saw to all the catering arrangements so that the women were entirely free, and the older girls took charge of the small children. The six days were concentrated on the gospel and its message with many familiar illustrations from the special missioner which appealed to women. The fan used by the country women for winnowing grain was a favourite and telling illustration on the manner in which the wheat and the chaff would be separated by God.

Six years later another mission in Hwochow had no need of a special missioner with her helpers. The evangelistic band of Hwochow was strong enough to speak for itself on the day when the local idol procession brought out thousands of spectators. Mildred's young people went into action as she herself had done years before in North London.

At the dispensary door there was always a long line of patients complaining always of two sorts of illness, "Fire" and "Chill". There was the child with the scalded arm who had been treated with rat oil and charred matting; the girl who said she had lost her eyesight through crying all day, and always the group of wan-looking people suffering from the "hundred days illness", the scourge of tuberculosis.

*   *   *

As she sat in her little study, an oasis in the middle of all the busy life of the Hwochow station, Mildred Cable looked back over the years which had made her dream come true. She and Evangeline French, now joined by Francesca French, were seeing some of the fruits of the harvest they had sown in the towns and villages of Shansi. The Revolution of 1911 had brought with it a big swing towards all the ways of the west, and missionaries, education, hospitals were popular. Unchanging China was in revolution, and the long years of feudal life were passing.

For twenty years and more the friends had worked hard in one place. They began to believe that God was calling them to take a new road of adventure for Him, out beyond the ranges of the hills of Shansi towards the far north-west, over the roof of the world, over the Gobi Desert.

They believed that God was calling them to leave their settled life at Hwochow, their schools and their friends, and no longer to have a home except one by the wayside. For twelve months they waited to be sure of God's guidance until in 1923 the way opened clear and certain for them to go forth and preach along the trade route across the Gobi Desert. For Mildred Cable, as the cart rattled out of Hwochow with her Bibles and her bed-roll, it was another part of her dream come true.

2

BEYOND THE GREAT WALL

IT was a lovely summer morning on June 11, 1923, when Mildred Cable and her two friends set out in their travelling cart to take the great road which led beyond the Great Wall of China into the Gobi Desert. That road was to be their home and familiar companion for the next fifteen years as they became travellers for God along the oldest trade route in the world.

Dressed in Chinese fashion with blue cotton coat, black silk skirt and stitched cotton hat, Mildred Cable led the way into the high cart. The three of them had to crawl in and sit amongst the boxes and the packages on the rough floor. The mules which had been cooped up in the stable were restive, kicking their hoofs on the stones, anxious to be off. The old cart with its high wheels and rough hooded roof looked unsteady and dangerous as it rolled away from the Hwochow Mission, away from the life the three friends had led, into the unknown.

That night they slept in a stable, just a cave hollowed out in the side of a cliff with a mud-built *kang*, a brick bed, heated in winter to keep travellers warm. The place was black with dirt, and in a recess was an alcove in which three men were lying, sleeping off the effects of opium smoking. It was a bitterly cold night, and with no heat in the *kang* the three friends slept very little. They could hear the mules chewing their food, and down there amongst them was their carter who was to guide them along the road. It was a dark, cold beginning to their great adventures for Christ. But as they lay there in the filth and blackness it seemed to Mildred Cable that this stable was probably very much like the one in which Jesus was born. She had no regrets when the dawn came and the cart rumbled along the stony road to the north-west.

*   *   *

Seven days to Lanchow, capital of Kansu, another seven to Liangchow, the road wound endlessly on across the sweeps of the bare hills, along the dry bed of an ancient inland sea. The bed was filled with the finest sand, and every drop of water in the area was very salt. Liangchow was the last missionary outpost of the China Inland Mission, the last certainty of a comfortable night's rest. The cart bumped on, from early morning until after dark. For in spite of the early morning start (never later than 4 a.m.) the travellers rarely got to their rest before nightfall.

On one early morning start Mildred Cable saw

ahead of them as they walked in front of the cart (their plan when travelling to get a time for quiet and meditation) a young woman who got off her donkey to look at them. She inspected them closely before speaking. She saw that their feet had never been bound in the Chinese style, but their dress was Chinese.

Could they read? Had they got husbands? How many children had they? Who would look after them when they got old?

The questions poured out from the young woman who had just come from a temple where she had been praying that she might bear a child. It gave Mildred Cable her opportunity to speak of the worship of the One True God, a Heavenly Father who provides for His people. It was a passing moment, a chance encounter, and the woman soon turned her donkey away from the main track. But the seed had been sown, and in many instances where the chance acquaintance could read a portion of Scripture was produced from the box of Bibles in the cart. Sometimes it was sold, and sometimes given.

*   *   *

By March 1924 the three friends were in the city of Kanchow, fifteen hundred miles away from Hwochow. The little cart had rumbled, and jolted, sometimes up to its axles in mud, and sometimes bogged down in swamps, but it had brought them along the road, strange vagrant creatures always eager to move on to the next place and never too tired to get there.

But Kanchow, the city where Marco Polo was once Governor, beautifully situated with its lakes and hosts of temples in their private gardens, attracted crowds of visitors, and the arrival of Mildred Cable and her two companions stirred the little Christian community in the city to an evangelistic campaign. A large tent was made, big enough to hold three hundred people, and with a band of eighteen students Mildred Cable led the company in witnessing and preaching. The tent was white, and gay with flags and bright Scripture posters, and soon the music of the baby organ and the sound of hymn singing drew a crowd of spectators. All the strange figures of the great road were there. Bearded Moslems, Turkis with turbans, Tibetans and Mongols listened to the addresses in Chinese which they all understood, and afterwards they were given Scripture portions in the language they could read. In the evening young soldier recruits came into the courtyard and enjoyed singing "Onward Christian Soldiers".

Going home one day after the campaign Mildred Cable was walking along the road thinking over the next move in the long trek to where the Great Wall ended, when a Turkestan Moslem caught her up. He was riding his donkey, and carried in his hand a number of Christian booklets. He stopped. Mildred was sitting by the roadside, by the edge of a poppy field blooming in brilliant colour, with the soft light of the landscape throwing a silvery glow over the scene.

"You are tired," he said. "I saw you in the tent yesterday. Perhaps you have no money to hire a donkey to get you home. Please use mine."

*　　*　　*

Away to the west from Kanchow lay Tibet. That mysterious land always fascinated Mildred Cable, so she and her friends were glad to go a three days' journey towards the far hills to visit a Tibetan Lamasery where the monks had given the Christians of Kanchow hospitality. So, loading the cart with books and a supply of rice and flour, the three set out and soon came to a wide and treacherous river. The mules and the cart plunged into the stream, which was sweeping along carrying mud and stones in a swift current. It looked a most dangerous crossing as the three friends sitting in the cart, with the water rushing underneath the boards, kept their eyes on the distant bank, while the mules struggled and swam valiantly in the river. They were almost over after an hour's anxious fording when one mule slipped and fell into deep water, and threatened to carry the other mules and the cart with him. But the team held themselves in the current, recovered their balance and clambered up the bank.

Mildred Cable was always full of gratitude to her animal friends, the donkeys and the mules which saw her up and down the great road during all the years of travelling. They were on the whole sensible beasts, and sturdy workers, and those two qualities always pleased her.

That night it was a Christian farmhouse which gave a great welcome. Rooms had been swept and prepared, and bowls of hot milk and fried doughnuts were ready on arrival. A sheep was killed, and the whole company sat down to a feast of mutton, vegetables and hot steamed bread.

To reach the Lamasery the travellers transferred themselves and their packages to donkeys with pack-saddles. On through a narrow gorge, mounting higher at every step, a whole day's journey into the mountains brought them just over the border into Tibet. They slept in a tiny hay-barn, and then next morning came out into a sunny Alpine valley with gentians, edelweiss and blue iris carpeting the ground.

The wind in the valley fluttered the prayer flags and the flowing stream turned the prayer wheels, and in the distance lay the low buildings of the Lamasery, from which rushed a group of red-robed Lamas and Living Buddhas to welcome the visitors. The large tent was soon up, and Mildred Cable was surrounded by inquisitive groups of Tibetan women who fingered her hair, examined her hands and tried on her hat. A wrist-watch which showed the time in the dark caused great excitement, and it was proved not to be a trick by a group huddling together under thick red shawls and forming a temporary dark-room. News of the wonder spread to the Lamasery and the wrist-watch was borrowed for the night.

There followed days of religious dancing with processions of priests, and as every rider came into the courtyards of the Lamasery he brought his gifts of meat, butter, and cheese. The three friends watched the celebrations with fascinated interest as the priests did their ceremonial dances dressed in magnificent satin robes with huge black masks with yawning mouths and bulging eyes. Presiding over it all was a Living Buddha, immobile, dignified, but yet watching every move. Down by the stream was the white tent of the visitors and crowds of the pilgrims came to it drawn by the strains of the organ and the hymn singing of the Chinese Christians.

*   *   *

So back again from this glimpse of Tibet to the high road to the north-west, where the great city of Suchow was the next stopping place. This journey was done purposely at a slow pace, not more than six miles a day, so that conversations and stops would not upset the programme. After all, time on this high road to the gateway to the Gobi Desert was not nearly so important as it was in other places. There must be time for talk and visits. In the tiny walled city of Fuyi rumour had spread the news of the three strange women who could speak Chinese and yet were not Chinese, and at the gateway of the Tu family home a crowd of fifty women and children came out to inspect them. The oldest woman was deputed to sit at table with the visitors, to watch their manners, and to discover why it was they had left their own homes and families to make the long journey. It was finally agreed that "spiritual merit" was the sole reason for their journey and with that the doors of friendship began to open.

In the Tu family one of the young men and his wife were already interested in the Christian faith, much to the anger of his mother. "The day you join the Christians," she said, "you may order my coffin, for I will not live to endure such a disgrace."

Her son answered his mother, "There is a way of life and a way of death. My path is that of Life."

When Mildred Cable was next in Fuyi she heard that Mr. Tu had braved the opposition of his mother and his family and had conducted Christian

worship in the town, and like a miracle in the days
of Christ all the people wondered at it.

Mile after mile, sometimes riding in the cart,
sometimes walking on foot through the fine sand
or on the hard stones, the travellers came nearer
to the famous city of Suchow, The Spring of
Wine as its people called it. Carrying their food
of carrots, celery, potatoes, egg-plant and onions
they felt more confident of not starving along the
road where the villages were scattered, and where
it was more than a day's journey between the
towns. How soon a once busy place might be lost
in the calamities of the climate was seen in a ruined
city called Camel Town. Its massive clay walls
were slowly falling away, and in the deserted
temple courts the clay images of the gods looked
grotesque and frightening. This city, buried under
the drifting sand, had become a halting place for
the camel caravans which moved along the road
with big bells round the camels' necks swinging
and ringing as they moved. To Mildred Cable's
surprise the head camel-man came forward and
spoke in educated Chinese, and after a cup of tea
he was pleased to accept bound copies of the
gospels and a bundle of Christian leaflets. For
fifty days he had been on the road, and he was
delighted to have something to read as he sat on
the leader-camel directing the caravan on its slow
march out of the Gobi southwards to the rich

cities of China. As she watched the caravan disappear over the horizon into the dim, purple distance Mildred Cable knew that the word of God, travel where it will, always speaks to the heart and life of the listener or the reader. It could never fail.

*   *   *

For ten months the three friends made their home in Suchow in a courtyard granted to them by a Chinese gentleman. It was the pavilion of his flower-garden, made of delicate fretwork and white paper, standing in the sun with glorious views of the Tibetan snow mountains. It was a one-roomed pavilion with a floor of loosely beaten earth, with no ceiling, but a high roof of pinewood rafters. Occupying the corners of the pavilion as little "bed-sitters", the friends shared the big central portion.

"The Christians have come"; so spread the news through the streets of Suchow, down through the smithies' street where the magnificent horses were shod, up past the Buddhist grand temple with its colossal Warrior-Guardians and crude models of the body and soul passing through the torments of the Underworld. "The Christians have come!" Mildred Cable looked at the feeble forces of herself and her friends, and then looked at the city preparing for a great theatrical festival. She began immediately to organize the little Christian group in the city. All the books and tracts they had brought were tied up in scarlet paper; the men went out for a two hours' period of preaching in the streets. Every shopkeeper was visited, and every restaurant too, with the request that they should exhibit one of the pretty floral posters. The women's group set off on a house-to-house visitation talking with the women in their homes, and the conversations usually began something like this: "You are a good needlewoman. Where did you learn that fancy stitch?" The three friends were inspected with astonishment and were asked the most awkward questions. "Did they wear skirts every day? How does she stick those glasses on her nose?" This pince-nez was a particular curiosity and never failed to open up a free and lively conversation. All Suchow soon knew that the Christians had come.

One winter's night a magnetic wind roared in from the mountains and plains round the city. It stripped every leaf from the trees, broke all the paper windows of the frail pavilion, and spread a thick layer of dust on everything. When the friends looked round their room and then at themselves they saw nothing but dust. No rain had fallen, but in its place a storm of dust had drowned the city. With the Gobi Desert on the west, and the sands of Mongolia to the north, Suchow was unprotected against such a deluge. It was the first taste of the high winds of the desert and of the terrible power of sand blown by the wind. Each of them added a layer of camel's hair to their wadded Chinese garments, and used the thick brown paper in which the Bibles were packed to paste over the cracks in the paper windows.

It was a cold, cold winter in Suchow, with the temperature dropping to fifteen degrees below zero. But every day the friends went into the city with their Bibles and tracts, talking to the people and letting them know that the Christians were still there in "The Spring of Wine". They lived very simply, with a midday dinner of rice or macaroni with plenty of good vegetables and eggs. For several months there was no cooking fat except a rancid kind of linseed oil which they could not stomach. They ground their own flour from a store of wheat, and in the bran they placed their eggs to prevent them from freezing.

As winter gave way to spring they ventured out on journeys to nearby towns in preparation for the long trek they knew must come in the summer. One trip was to Kinta, city of the Golden Tower, whose dome was at one time sheathed in pure gold. There the temple was crowded by young brides beseeching the gods for the gift of a son, and by the mothers of children who had come to return thanks. Covered by a red scarf, the baby was held under an immense iron bell while the mother offered up a handkerchief full of grain. As the bell clanged, the priest took some of the grain and scattered it over the child's face with the words, "May the Goddess of Mercy protect thee; may the God of Plenty endow thee." Then yellow paper was burnt and its ashes smeared over the child's forehead, and the mother went away happy at the thought that everything had been done to safeguard the child's future.

Another trip was to the "Halls of Learning", twenty miles outside Suchow, where hundreds of shrines on the mountain-side drew thousands of pilgrims each year. Here the white tent was pitched, and the hymn singing drew a crowd of the curious who learned about another way of life, free from the fear of demons and the power of death.

*　　*　　*

Then came the day in August 1925 when the friends started their great journey which was to lead them beyond the Great Wall, over the Gobi Desert, and through the cities of Central Asia. Their new cart was made entirely of wood without a piece of iron or even a nail. Its great wooden wheels were eight feet high, which could carry it through the rivers and across seas of mud, and its hood was thatched with grass. In place of a mule a horse was bought, one already hardened to road travel. Packed once more with food, sleeping bags, boxes of Bibles and books the party waved farewell as the cart rolled out on to the road with its vast wheels turning in the hot sun and leaving their impress on the dust.

Twenty miles down the road, or rather up the road, for the pull was always upwards to the Gobi, they saw the rising towers of Kiayiukwan built at the narrowest point between the hills at the end of the Great Wall of China. Dating back to 214 B.C., the Great Wall was built to protect China against the tribes of the outer world, the world of terror and mystery the three friends were going to visit. Here, through a single gateway in the huge wall, dominated with a turret, passed all the human traffic of distant Asia. Criminals, prodigals, outlaws and pilgrims all made for the gate of Kiayiukwan, called the "Mouth of China". The three friends were at last passing through the mouth, and they were naturally excited as the huge cart (which had cost them fifty shillings to make) crossed the bridge into the city and turned into the courtyard of "The Inn of Harmonious Brotherhood".

"Turn in, turn in," called the inn-keeper.

"Have you grass for the horse?"

"Plenty and at a fair price."

How often they were to hear that dialogue on the road across the Gobi. Here they were beyond the Great Wall, the end and the beginning of their venture for God in Central Asia.

3

ACROSS THE GOBI

GOBI! The name had fascinated Mildred Cable for years, and now that she and her friends were on the threshold of the vast, bare, stony waste stretching on for a thousand miles across Central Asia they were the more eager to meet people who had crossed it.

Just outside the gate of Kiayiukwan Mildred climbed a high stony mound erected by the simple guardians of the gate to keep off the evil spirits of the Gobi.

"There are demons in the Gobi, lady," they said; "the place is full of them."

"Do many people get lost in the desert?" Mildred asked.

"Yes, very many. They miss their way and die of thirst, and some are frozen to death in winter blizzards. Must you go to the Gobi, lady?"

"I must go," said Mildred, "because I am seeking the lost and some of them are out there."

The soldier's eyes lit up. He thought he understood at last the purpose of these three strange women who had come to the Gate of the Demons with their cart and were setting out all alone across the desert. They were looking for someone lost. He had often heard of parents sending out a son to find another who was lost. Perhaps this was the plan of these travellers.

"I know I shall find them," said Mildred, "for God who is their God and mine will lead me to them."

The soldier listened in silence. These "holy women" he thought would surely come safely through the perils of the Gobi. He was even more sure when on the day the cart rumbled through the gateway on its long journey the travellers threw stones against the walls of Kiayiukwan. All travellers did this. If the stones rebounded then all would be well.

All three threw stones. They rebounded from the wall with an echo like the cheeping of chicks.

"That's the echo of the spot," grinned the soldiers. "You're lucky to hear it. All will be well."

* * *

The little cart was well loaded with boxes of books, Bibles and tracts, which on the uphill road made the horse pull heavily. So Mildred walked in her Chinese cotton shoes over the rough stony track in order to get the "feel" of the Gobi. By five o'clock in the afternoon she looked back to the towers of Kiayiukwan in the fading light of the approaching sunset. The road soon lay in shadow

35

and the icy breath of the coming night made her shiver. She pulled her thick wadded Chinese coat round her, and scrambled up into the cart where the others were preparing to keep warm during the night. In order to make the first stages easy for the horse and themselves and the carter they decided to travel by night when the air was cool and they would not get so thirsty, for there was no water for long distances.

On through the night the cart creaked, and in the deep silence they could hear the steady padding of the feet of the horse and of the carter too as he walked by its side. Mildred sat awed by the vast starry expanse of the Gobi sky as it hung like an immense velvet canopy with great golden lights. About midnight the moon rose, and its soft light seemed to deepen the silence. There was nothing to move, not a blade of grass, not a tree leaf, not an insect or a bird. On each side of the stony track spread the waving, dark landscape of the Gobi. The little cart and its travellers seemed so lonely and forgotten.

Suddenly out of the night came the ringing of bells. It was the mail rider carrying the post across the Gobi. He, too, rode by night, spurring his horse over the lonely miles from stage to stage, mounting a fresh horse at every stop. When she later met the post-rider in a village he joked to Mildred Cable about the weight of the mail he had to carry, all because of the books and letters which the Christians sent to and fro.

At sunrise they reached the village they had been making for, and the weary travellers flung their coverlets on the mud bed of the inn and were soon fast asleep. A few hours' deep sleep was always enough to refresh Mildred Cable and soon she was out walking about the village street talking to the tradesmen. In one little shop she noticed a jar of coarse, grey sand.

"What do you keep sand for?" she asked. "Isn't there enough of it all round to be had for nothing?"

"This is special sand, lady," said the shopkeeper. "It is so heavy that it does not blow about, and it's the sand used for polishing jade. It's hard, but it never scratches the surface."

Four days later the cart rolled beneath the light elegant tower of Jade Gate, the lovely name of the city of Yumen where they stayed a few days. Since a hundred years before Christ the Jade Gate had been one of the ways for all travellers across the Gobi to pass through. The visit of "The Holy Women" brought a crowd of people to look at them in the inn. One old lady believed that they would know the secrets of all the happenings, and could tell her what things were lost and who stole them. She whispered to Mildred Cable, "Please tell me the name of the thief who stole my cow."

*   *   *

As they rumbled on by night, sleeping in the village inns for a few hours by day, and then walking about the little towns to see and to be seen, the travellers were in no hurry. They had lived long enough in China to know that time does not matter, and that in the little towns of the Gobi borderlands they could only witness for Christ if they had plenty of time and plenty of good-humoured patience.

Every town had its particular demons and legends. At Pulungki, out beyond the Jade Gate, the folk believed that their city was the original Garden of Eden where the human race began. Beneath the stony soil were caves heaped with treasures, and any hole in the ground might be the entrance to a robber's den or a wonderful grotto piled high with gems. Men had tried to dig for the treasures, but when the secret was about to be tapped a gust of cold wind and the flapping of wings drove them back. Fear and terror ruled the lives of the people, and as Mildred Cable watched the endless miles go slowly by as the patient horse pulled them higher and higher on to the Gobi plateau she did not wonder that many of the Gobi people were frightened at the world they lived in.

In one inn a gift was awaiting them on arrival. News spread mysteriously in the Gobi lands, and the gift was from an old woman who had heard that the three "Preachers of Righteousness" were arriving and she wished to show them a kindness. Her gift was two small cabbages, three turnips and a little vinegar. Mildred Cable went to see her in her miserable hovel. She was living alone trying by purity of actions to please her gods. She wanted to know from the Preachers about "The Way of Life" and so eager was she to learn that she called in a young man to help her remember what the Preachers said, and to follow their instructions. She listened to the story of Jesus, and learned a little prayer by heart, and on the morning of the friends' departure she was up to meet them at daybreak with her face washed, her hair combed, all done in honour of the Great God they had told her about.

Not everyone, however, along the Gobi road realized their purpose so clearly. In one village where they stayed to preach and distribute literature they were surprised one night to see a crowd of fifty people gathered round an old gentleman who was speaking about the visitors. They recognized him as the old schoolmaster who had come to the meetings and listened most intently. With his horn-rim spectacles and his old purple gown and long plait of hair he was respected by the community as the man who always knew the truth about what was happening. Who were these women? He knew. He had read their books and understood their religion. They had been sent to Gobi by the King of Europe. He was paying their expenses, for ever since the war there was a shortage of girls in Europe. The young men were clamouring for brides, and the three women had come to Gobi to get them. As the old man finished his explanation Mildred Cable came up to the back of the crowd, and there was general laughter when they all saw that she had heard and understood the explanation.

*　　*　　*

On towards Ainsi they were moving towards the border of China proper, nearer to Turkestan where the Gobi had the name of Black Gobi. As she looked at the expanse of the desert from the North Gate of Ainsi Mildred Cable saw a sea of small black pebbles mixed with grey grit, as unpromising as anything she had yet seen along the road. Travelling by night to avoid the burning heat by day, the travellers found the road more lonely than any of the other stretches. The black, grey Gobi seemed to be uninhabited except in the few villages, and there was one oasis which had a spring of water gushing from a cliff, running into a little canal and so watering a patch of earth and turning it green. Mildred Cable loved the little oases. In this one a few lonely families were tilling the poppy fields and making a living out of opium.

She and her friends visited every family and told them of the love of Christ and left behind literature for the long, cold winter nights.

It was along this lonely stretch of Black Gobi that the travellers passed what seemed to be a heap of sheepskins by the roadside, but a little stick by its side showed that something living and human was beneath the heap. The carter stirred the heap, and slowly a man's parched mouth opened and murmured, "Water." Mildred and her friends got down from the cart and held a cup to his lips, and he whispered, "Water, and I am your slave for life." The man was plainly very ill and too weak to walk. They had no water to leave with him, and they had no time to spare to stay with him. Besides, if they took him he might die on the way, and the carter did not want a dead man on his hands. It would lead to serious trouble. But Mildred and her friends at once said they could not leave a sick man by the roadside. One of them would walk by the cart so that the man could ride, and so they brought the man to the next inn where as at the Inn of the Good Samaritan the inn-keeper cared for him. In a few days he was well again and proved to be an educated young man from far distant China who had come to secure a good post in those remote parts of his country. He knew that his life had been saved, for the Gobi road every year took its toll of travellers who died of thirst, and he was full of gratitude to the little party in the cart.

It was always the custom of the travellers when staying at an inn to have family worship, and they were often joined by other guests. One Moslem gentleman travelling with his suite attended, and when the Scriptures were read they all bowed their heads and joined in the prayers for safety on the roads. On another occasion the arrival of the travellers with the harmonium and parcels of books broke up the gambling rings of a group of soldiers, who then gladly spent their money on the gaily bound Testaments.

Waiting to cross the border into Turkestan was a weary business, but to Mildred Cable wherever there were people there was an opportunity to speak about the Christian faith, and when at last the message came to give them permission to proceed the soldiers of the border garrison turned out to wish them a good journey, and an officer's wife even sent down a present of two cucumbers and a melon. As these were luxuries in the stony black Gobi it was a generous gift and represented a whole day's ration for her household.

* * *

The permission to travel was addressed to the officials in stately style and informed them that the three ladies, "Feng Precious Pearl, Feng

Polished Jade and Kai All Brave" were people of
the highest reputation and could cross the border
into Turkestan without delay.

By this time—for they had been on the road,
up and down it, for nearly three years—they
had got accustomed to the roadside inns, and
even liked those rooms where there were no
windows. Travelling by night in the cart they
had plenty of air and quiet, and by day they
could sleep almost anywhere. At the village of
Dove Tower the room was so dark that no flies
ever got through to it, and the mud walls so thick
that no heat from the sun ever entered. The wind
and the sand of the Gobi were kept out too.

And so with the mules' noses (for the horse
had been exchanged for mules in this edition of
what Mildred called "The Gobi Express") set
for distant Urumchi five hundred miles away the
travellers settled to the long grind of travelling,
talking, teaching, preaching and distributing.
Sometimes it was only a three mile trek, sometimes
six, but they knew that it was three weeks to the
great city.

One of the many surprises on the way was the
wonderful city of Hami with its new inn where
the windows were newly papered, and there was
fresh clean matting on the floors. What a feast it
was on the first night—most of it cooked by
Mildred and her friends themselves in the inn

kitchen on condition that they did not use any pork, lard or swine's flesh. There was rice and good fresh bread, a dish of chopped mutton and egg-plant fried together, a plate of French beans in mutton fat with sliced cucumber, and plenty of "sweet water" tea followed by slices of cantaloupe melon.

It was lovely to live for a few days in Hami with its fine parks, wide canals stretching away for seven miles to the north and five to east and west; one of the biggest oases the travellers had seen in the Gobi. As usual they went to see the landlord's family, for he had four wives each living in her own courtyard. The girls of the family wore gay dresses made in one piece, slit at the neck by a hole, and always worn right down to the ankle. A veil of white muslin covered the head and fell to the knees. In many of the Hami homes the travellers were able to talk with the women in Chinese, and in some they left gospels in Arabic. Through the bazaars they saw the trading and bargaining of Asia in fine cottons, silks, carpets and rugs, while down through the streets walked the handsome Turki merchants and sometimes a tall, pale woman balancing a water pot on her head.

The road had now brought them into Asia and also to the Great Heat of the Gobi. Slowly they mounted by night to over five thousand feet to the foothills of the Barkul Mountains, and by day sweltered in the heat which here seemed to penetrate into even the darkest inn. At Kucheng it was suggested they might take the Governor's Express Cart for the last stage to Urumchi, but when they saw the wild horses careering with it along the road they preferred the slow safe trudge of the mule cart. Besides, they could now go by day, for the road was easier and there was more water for the animals.

At Urumchi they were some seven hundred miles from the Russian border and the worst of the Gobi journey was over. Molly, one of the mules, was happily installed in the stable of the Urumchi Mission house, and the travellers went on to the Russian border in a cart called a tarantass. Friends in the city provided a huge box of food for the seven hundred miles of road which lay ahead. The tarantass was galloped out of Urumchi at six miles an hour, double the pace of the Gobi, and in a fortnight with jingling of bells they were at the Russian border, which to Mildred and her friends seemed very nearly home. By October (1926) they had crossed the breadth of Russia itself and were in London with the breathless story of having crossed the Gobi on their lips.

4

GOBI CITIES AND OASES

MILDRED CABLE loved to be on the go,
and that meant the almost as exciting job
of planning the journey. So in March 1928 when
she and her friends left London to travel again
on the Gobi road they hoped to enter by the door
of Turkestan, but the way through Russian terri-
tory was forbidden. Difficulties were made only
to be overcome by Mildred Cable, and the change
of plan took the trio through India to the foothills of the Himalayas, and then across the ocean
to Shanghai, and up the great river to Hankow
and so northwards and westwards to their old
headquarters at Suchow.

They enjoyed every minute of the months of
travel, and they were specially excited when they
got to Lin-Tung in China where the water bubbles
up from the ground hot and sulphurous. Nothing
would satisfy Mildred except a dip in the swim-
ming tank where the sulphur fumes infected the
water and gave it a refreshing quality. So, giving
a reward to the attendant to keep away the bands
of curious children, the three friends swam in the
tank and came out invigorated, leaving behind the

dust and grime of the road. A large notice by the side of the bath read, "Hearts may here be washed clean."

This time on the Gobi Road they had a new cart with camel-hair cover, wadded lining, and— most ingenious of all—a "window" so arranged that the pane of glass showed them everything that was happening outside without being seen themselves inside. The cart also had a pair of ears which stood out on either side, and had nets for carrying the flour bag, the frying-pan, the carter's sheepskin and the parcels of tracts. This time they had lamps, too, for the evangelistic tent, plenty of paraffin oil to light them, and a tent for themselves.

* * *

Mildred was always ready to go off to interesting places away from the track, for her inquiring mind and observant eye were alert to the beauty and the history of the Gobi. One excursion was to the Caves of the Thousand Buddhas, which she called "the art gallery of the Gobi". Hidden far away behind the sand dunes, with its story going back to over two hundred years before Christ, the Caves were cut in the face of the cliff, and each one of the openings was the entrance to a temple or shrine. All the walls were covered with paintings and designs, and the colours glowed in the warm light of the Gobi. All round the caves the old Abbot Wang had made a green oasis with a running stream, fresh young poplar trees and green grass. As Mildred walked through these silent halls with their roofs decorated in intricate patterns, the walls richly painted in designs which seemed to have no beginning or ending, she meditated on the thousand years and more the Caves had been there.

The Abbot had prepared a guest-house with clean sleeping rooms, and to get the money for the building he had gone on a begging tour to the towns and the farms, and rarely came home empty handed. His friendliness won Mildred Cable's heart, and when years later she came again to the Caves she was saddened to hear of his death, and to be led to his tomb where he slept with the age-old wonders he had so lovingly looked after.

She saw some craftsmen busy on the face of the cliffs. They were chipping away the face of the cliff to make room for a colossal Buddha who was to be placed there, eighty feet high, looking out over the desert, silently presiding over the dunes, the wind, and the waving poplar trees. As Mildred watched the men chipping away the ancient cliff, making a niche for the Buddha, she realized that the workmen had not the skill of the artists who had painted the walls of the ancient halls. Their Buddha was rather an ugly idol, and

she wondered whether the gracious spirit of the
Caves was changing under modern conditions;
she longed to preach in those old temples the
Good News of the One True God.

*　　*　　*

As they talked and preached their way in the
oasis of Tunhwang they often heard of the Lake
of the Crescent Moon hidden behind the lofty
sand dunes.

"You see, lady," said one man to Mildred, "the
Caves of the Buddhas were made by man, but the
Lake of the Crescent Moon is god's handiwork."

"But how far is it?" asked Mildred.

"Just behind the range of the sandhills. It is
more beautiful than words can tell."

Mildred knew how deceptive distances were in
the Gobi. She often looked towards those sandhills. They seemed so near, and when the light
shone on their sloping sides they came so close as
to be almost in the town.

"It's only four miles, lady, and when you get
there you'll find water, clean guest-rooms and a
quiet place to rest."

It might be only four miles to the lovely Lake
of the Crescent Moon, but when she and her
friends started off to see the lake they knew it
would be more like eight miles. At every step they
sank up to their ankles in the sands, ploughing up-

wards across the sandhills, and as they got to the top it was exhausting to lift their legs up to take the next step. Each ridge of sand seemed to lead no to another, but at last the top was reached, and over the edge Mildred Cable looked down to one of the loveliest sights she had seen in the Gobi.

Down there lay the lake, small, crescent-shape and sapphire blue, enclosed by the tinted brown sand. The easiest way down to it was to slide through the sands. So they did, and as they slid the sands joined in the fun with a singing noise. It was like the twanging of a gigantic musical instrument, and it echoed all round the lake.

"It's our thunder," said the priest at the little temple by the lake shore. "You will often hear it whenever the wind blows on the spot you came down. You struck the exact place to make the sands speak."

That was a happy thought for the days the trio spent at the beautiful lake. But it could also be a grim, forbidding place, as Mildred discovered when she came to it once in mid-winter. The lake was frozen and bitter winds swept over its surface, and the sand dunes had the hard look of places where no human being could live. But at every season of the year there was always a pilgrim or two at the Lake. One man she met there wore two mirrors fixed above his forehead, for he believed that with them he could see both the past and the future. He called himself "The Messenger of Peace to all nations" and when Mildred spoke to him about the Prince of Peace he listened long and patiently. His life was spent going from one Lamasery to another, and round his broad-brimmed hat was draped a passport to Lhasa in far-away Tibet which it was his ambition to visit. When Mildred gave him a copy of the gospels in his language he thanked her, and said he must tell her story to all the Lamas he met.

Another pilgrim arrived at the lake guest-house in bare feet.

"Where have you come from, Lama?" Mildred asked.

"From the Utai Mountain in Shansi. I have been walking for six months." His red and yellow robes were soiled and dirty, his feet torn and black. At every few steps in the long journey he prostrated himself on the earth. It was all done, he said, to fulfil a vow.

Mildred gave him a copy of St. John's Gospel which he opened at the first page and read the words, *"In the beginning was the Word, and the Word was with God, and the Word was God."*

"It's about Jesus," he said. His face lit up. "I know I will have to believe him."

So the pilgrims of the Gobi parted there at the Lake of the Crescent Moon. The seed of the Good

News had been sown, and Mildred and her friends knew that through wayside conversations like that God would stir the hearts of people to believe. The Lake and the Thunder of the Sands and the trudge through the hills had had their reward.

*   *   *

As the cart carried most things the travellers needed it was not often necessary to go to a shop to buy, but when they did Mildred enjoyed the occasion so much that she called it a social event. One day the three friends wished to buy some Chinese silk and three face towels in the city of Hami. On arriving at the shop the merchant at once served tea, and his assistants scurried round to bring the goods to the counter. The conversation started about things nothing to do with the business in hand, as the merchant most politely wanted to know about London, about England, and only casually mentioned that all his pieces of silk were good pieces.

Meanwhile Mildred's sharp eye was looking at every inch of the silk for uneven threads, which so impressed the crowd which had invaded the shop that they murmured, "They know about everything." The silk was weighed and the face towels selected, and then the real business of bargaining began.

Looking at the price tag Mildred smiled and

offered half the price, but the courteous merchant merely smiled and pointed to a notice outside his shop which said, "No prices discussed here," to which all the crowd echoed, "He does not discuss prices."

Long years of life in China had taught Mildred that this was only the prelude to a happy settlement between shopkeeper and customer, so she smiled again and ceased to bargain, and merely assured everybody that her money was not enough to pay for such expensive articles.

"Have a little more tea," smiled the merchant; "you are our guests from a far country"—a sure sign that the bargain was settled. Paper was produced, ink was brought and the merchant started to write out the account. Bringing out a piece of paper from her pocket Mildred, too, added up the figures, to the astonishment of the crowd which watched her nimble fingers flying over the paper. "Did you see that?" asked one man. "Reading, writing and arithmetic all come quite easy to them!" Everybody was happy at the purchase, and as Mildred left she presented the merchant with a packet of Christian books.

It was part of the evangelistic plan of the trio to stay for days and even weeks in a big city like Hami, meeting the people and seizing every chance of commending the gospel by service to them. A young man came running to them one day saying that his wife had poisoned herself and the only remedy he could think of was to give her mare's milk. Mildred's medical skill was known by this time up and down the Gobi road, so out came the medicine box, and in an hour the young woman's life was put out of immediate danger.

"I thought you would come," said her husband, "for both of us used to attend your children's services at Suchow."

Simple instances of that kind were a deep reward for many weary days of travel, and so were more lengthy conversations with the learned people of the cities and oases. It was in Hami after a long talk with some Moslem visitors that one of them openly admitted, "Truly the Holy Man Jesus is coming soon, and he will rule the earth in righteousness."

There were always surprises round the corner in Gobi travel and Gobi conversations. A visit to the Temple of the Dragon King outside Hami started a talk with a Tibetan Lama in the temple. There in the cool of the temple park away from the heat and bustle of Hami the three friends were invited to tea by the Lama. The four chatted together about the crowds which came out from the city on festival days, and they asked,

"What do they hope to gain, Lama?"

"The forgiveness of their sins," he said.

The trio looked at him straightly and asked,

"Do you know of any way in which sins can be forgiven?"

The Lama looked at his visitors, these three strange, grey-haired women from the outside world who were holy and yet so practical, so kind and yet so eager to ask the pointed question. He confessed that he did not know any way of forgiveness.

For a long time they talked about the Christian way of forgiveness, saying that forgiveness was free, and that the way of work and good actions by men could not do all that God could do. The Lama listened politely, and the trio left to go home. Just another talk on the Gobi road, they thought. So it was, but in a few days' time a visitor was announced at their home in Hami. It was the Lama from the Temple of the Dragon King. From the folds of his robe he produced a packet of yellow silk which he unfolded and took out some paper money and handed it to the trio. "Here is a little money to help you with your good work."

* * *

A town off the main track was always a temptation to plan an expedition. And that was how they came to Barkul, lying away behind the snow peaks of the Barkul Mountains. It was the little daughter of the inn-keeper of Cart Wheel Spring who hopped on her donkey and led the cavalcade through the green sand, and past the desert rock gardens with flowers of crimson and yellow and russet. All these colours of the desert made Mildred's heart dance with delight. She loved the big spaces of the desert but also the minute details of rocks and flowers in the crannies and pockets of earth amidst the warm tinted stones.

Their little guide took them surely and firmly to Barkul, where the comments of the people at the inn were most amusing. "Books." "More Books." "Great Students." "They all wear glasses, for their eyes have been destroyed by so much reading." "How does the short one keep her glasses on with nothing over the ears to hold them?"

It was not always easy to find a way into the homes of the people in a new town where they were not known, but fortunately walking down the street Mildred spotted a familiar face. It was a young man who had come to the children's service in Suchow. He and his family were now in Barkul where his sister was married to the Commander of the garrison.

So unexpectedly in a strange city a door was opened for the preaching of the gospel through a young man who said that he had remembered to pray every day since the children's meetings at Suchow.

In one rich home in Barkul the trio talked with

an educated young woman who had been studying
the books and tracts the visitors had been selling.
She was a keen inquirer, but the background of
her life was dark and heavy with demon-worship,
as Mildred discovered when they were all invited
to celebrate the funeral ceremonies of the twenty-
first anniversary of her father's death. It was a
time of wailing and feasting, chanting and gambling, but the hostess on the arrival of her three
special guests ordered quietness, and in the middle
of the pagan orgy they heard the words about Jesus
and His resurrection and about the Life He gives
through His death.

And so on this journey the three friends gradually made their way over the Gobi road to Urumchi
for the winter months of November 1929 to Feb-
ruary 1930. Six stages out from Urumchi they
saw two travellers coming towards them, and one
of them waved his hat. He was a tall, silver-haired
man whom they immediately recognized as their
friend Percy Mather, a missionary from Urumchi.
What pleased the trio almost as much was to see
Molly the Mule, which had pulled the old cart so
many hundreds of miles. She was proudly carrying
Mr. Mather on her back, fit and well after her long
rest at Urumchi.

"Your nose, madam! Rub it quickly!" called
out a Russian to Mildred one day in the bitter
Urumchi winter. Mildred stroked it. Sure enough

it was dead. Frostbite. She rubbed very hard and gradually the circulation returned, and then a kind Russian woman rubbed in vodka too and soon Mildred had a warm, happy nose again. All through that winter they wore high felt socks and felt boots to keep their feet warm. Each day they set themselves to learn the Turki language, and plodded through the grey, snow-swept streets of the city to meet people and to give their witness for Christ. As the winter gave way to spring their thoughts turned again to the cities and oases of the Gobi.

5

FRIENDS AND FOES IN THE GOBI

THE Gobi Road was a friendly road but a dangerous one too. By the time Mildred Cable and her friends had gone up and down it five times they knew the bends and twists in the track and even where the cart would jolt, and where the longest stages would be. With Molly the Mule or with hired horses drawing the Gobi Express or the Flying Turki, the "Teachers of Righteousness" had the right of way, and never in the fifteen years of Gobi travel were they seriously interfered with, although often frightened.

All through the Chinese-speaking parts of the Gobi they were easily at home amongst their friends who spoke Chinese, but as the road led on into the Turki-speaking parts of Turkestan they had to learn another tongue. One of their teachers was a stalwart, bearded young man of twenty-three who most of the day sat selling cloth and home-made soap on the street. When he heard that there was money to be made by teaching the ladies Turki, Qurban jumped at the idea. But when his father heard about it he soundly beat him, for as a Moslem he must not help anyone to preach the Christian faith. But Qurban crept secretly through the garden of the little house, often hiding himself behind the trees while his father's spies looked for him. Finally he was arrested by the Head of the Mosque and was about to be cruelly beaten when a friend pleaded that he was poor and needed the money that the teachers paid. "If he promises not to teach them we will give him money," said the priest, so Qurban was given two hundred dollars, and it looked as if he would no longer teach Turki to the travelling missionaries. But he soon crept back through the garden and secretly taught, and listened too.

Then there was the cook who in October 1930 joined the friends in Suchow. Mildred looked him up and down, for he was a tall, big man, and by his side stood his tiny little son, a wee child in his little Chinese coat and trousers. He could cook but he also knew the road to Eye Lash Oasis, which made him doubly valuable. So he became "Sir Thomas Cook and Son" to the travellers, and how excellently he lived up to his famous name! Sir Thomas would often ride ahead to secure lodgings, and in Eye Lash itself he set up a temporary home in a courtyard because there was no inn in the town. The farmers in that part of the Gobi knew Sir Thomas and opened their homes to the ladies, and when camels were needed for a sandy stretch of the journey three beasts appeared from nowhere and meekly knelt to receive their loads, including Mildred and her friends perched on the bed-bags on their bony backs. Sir Thomas was never at a loss, and even when turned out of his kitchen he always managed to cook somewhere else and see that his ladies were fed.

When at Christmas 1931 they were all turned out of their home at Tunhwang Sir Thomas led them across to the Lake of the Crescent Moon to the guest-house by the lake, and trudged the miles to and fro with food for Christmas dinner. But on December 23 he arrived with the welcome news that the soldiers had gone, and that Christmas could be spent in the old home. So the carts were hurriedly packed with steaming bread, half cooked meat, clothes, books and kitchen pots, and guided by Sir Thomas the caravan trekked back to Tunhwang for Christmas where the never-defeated cook produced a Christmas dinner with tea and cake for all the Christians in the oasis.

Brother Chen was the general factotum for many journeys along the road. He had been a farm worker and had to be taught how to lay a table even when there was only one knife and a spoon for the three. Chopsticks for three were easily arranged, but only one knife and spoon?

Brother Chen learned that they could be put in the centre of the table, but it took a long time for him to see that they were for serving only. When Brother Chen had to cook he was far too lavish, but he never seemed to eat anything himself. His only bedding was his top coat and for a pillow he used a piece of firewood, but when pay day came Brother Chen's eyes lighted up, for his money usually went towards buying a handsome bound copy of the Scriptures in large type.

Mr. Bluff was a carter, one of the many carters who led the travelling carts along the road, but he was true to his name. Could he drive a cart? Of course he could. His head was swathed in the blue cotton head-dress of the professional, and therefore he knew all about mules and carts, how to feed the one and drive the other. He had good legs, too, for walking, and his baggage was only a large iron pot, a bag of sultanas and a wadded quilt. So Mr. Bluff started to drive his team on the Gobi Road, and the mules, fresh and restive after spending the winter in the stables, decided Mr. Bluff was no carter. Molly the Mule was the first to see through Mr. Bluff. She reared and kicked. Then the horses drawing the large cart were steered into a large hole in the road, and Molly was called on to help pull them out. In the darkness Mr. Bluff got Molly's traces wound round the axle and poor Molly was nearly strangled alive.

"Take your pot and go," shouted the company in the two carts; "this settles your account."

But Mr. Bluff was no ordinary carter. He tramped along singing to himself, and as the weeks passed by he was still there with his iron pot and bag of sultanas.

"Never again shall I see my home, never again, never again," he sang to himself, and the three friends had no heart to turn him away.

* * *

There were foes too in those days on the Gobi as the Russian influence across the borders of Turkestan, Mongolia and Siberia began to seep along the trade routes. One of them was the boy General Lei, just eighteen and known as "The Thunderbolt". His brigands rode one day into Suchow and with guns levelled at the trio demanded that they should produce their husbands. When they said they had no husbands to offer, the men with the guns only shouted the more, "Send them up here quick."

To parley with three women was beneath the dignity of the General's gunmen, so Mildred persuaded an old man-servant in the house to go up to the roof where the men were standing and ask what they wanted.

He returned with the one word "Money" on his lips.

The three friends stood there white-faced and anxious, looking up at the intruders on the flat roof. They had little money with them, but they knew that the whole city was in the hands of the brigands who were stealing food, money and anything else they could take away. So Mildred counted out their little stock of silver and handed it to the men, who slipped off the roof and away into the darkness.

A few days later a rider galloped along the Gobi Road with a message from General Lei. He demanded the presence of the three foreign women as soon as possible in the city of Ainsi, his headquarters. At first Mildred counselled "No". Nothing would induce her to take the long journey to Ainsi to see this turbulent brigand general who was making life so dangerous for everyone. But the sight of the mayor and the town councillors with such white faces and trembling lips, as they talked in whispers about what would happen to them if the trio did not go, made Mildred relent.

They were allowed to go in their own cart, and on a bleak November morning with the bitter wind of the Gobi sweeping across the road they set out. They knew it was four days' trek. To the right and left of the cart marched an armed escort, rough looking soldier-bandits with their guns ready for use. Behind the cart trudged a company of two hundred young men, many of them tied together with ropes, all of them prisoners, some of them destined for swift execution at the whim of the boy General they were going to see. Even the trio themselves, as they huddled together to keep warm, realized that they, too, were prisoners.

As they left the city the Christians watched them with fear and weeping. No one had yet come back alive from the General's camp. But the trio burst into a hymn in which all the Christians joined:

> *I am weak, but Thou art mighty,*
> *Hold me with Thy powerful hand!*

Chilled by the icy blasts of the winter winds, with no hot meals for four days, but only bread and tea, the three friends came into Ainsi tired, cold and hungry and with an inward fear in their hearts. What would this mad boy General do to them? Lodged in a schoolroom near his house they heard stories of the commandeering of every house in the town, and of all supplies of food and equipment. Summoned to the presence of "The Thunderbolt", they saw him sitting on a dais with handsome rugs spread around, and guns hanging on the walls. Round him stood the fiercest set of ruffians they had seen in all the Gobi—bearded, turbaned men with their hands on their guns ready to act and shoot at the slightest word of authority.

But "The Thunderbolt" himself looked an effeminate young man. He was tall and slender, and leaned back on the couch discussing how a man who had displeased him should be executed. He looked at Mildred and asked for some advice for an old gunshot wound which was troubling him. Would the treatment hurt? He thought the disinfectant would make the skin smart?

They were saddened as they listened to the conversation of this young man who had them in his power. Why had he brought them to his camp? Perhaps they were hostages against misfortune? Perhaps in a frenzy of bargaining with another war-lord he would pass them over like so much goods and chattels?

Day after day in the cold schoolroom they waited to hear their fate. Only a small ration of millet was given them for daily food, and there was no firewood for the brazier. Their great fear was a long detention, but they were also more afraid that if they mentioned their release it might make the General angry, and their stay indefinite.

At last came a chance to speak to the General's chief of staff, who spoke French. They boldly asked to be allowed to go home. To their amazement he came back with a permit. As boldness had accomplished this miracle they decided on boldness again when they came to say "Goodbye" to the General himself. As they stood in front of this fickle, upstart young man they said nothing about leaving, but carrying out the bold plan of the three Mildred stepped forward and handed him a copy of the New Testament and of the Ten Commandments. She spoke to him clearly and boldly about the care of his own soul. Looking down on these three valiant women the young man was silent. The bearded brigands gazed in wonder at their daring, and as they went out of the room the trio themselves wondered at what they had done.

* * *

Free from the brigand general they were still confined to the oasis by his orders, and for eight months they schemed and planned to escape northwards through his lines to the Turkestan border. For months they had been without sugar, tea, candles, soap and paraffin, and their meagre supply of grain was running short. Unless they could escape soon they would starve. So, secretly packing the carts by night, they arranged their flight. They left their room just as it was with tins on the table, pictures on the walls, a quilt on the bed and the brazier ready to be lit. Anyone peeping through the paper window would conclude they had just gone off for the day and would be back at night.

As the gates of the town opened in the early morning they slipped through to the south and then turned north away from the track across fields cut with channels for irrigation. It was hard going. The mules sweated and strained, and the cart rolled in the ditches so violently that it almost broke its axles. All day they pushed on, and it was past midnight with the morning star shining over the desert when the three lay down to sleep by the bank of a wide river they had to cross. Before they attempted to cross every strap and rope of the mules and carts had to be tested, for the only way to get over was to rush across quickly.

With a touch of the whip the mules gallantly braved the swirling torrent, and with yells from the driver struggled against the stream.

The three friends held on to the cart as it swayed in the water, praying that the sturdy cart would hold together and the mules find their feet again on firm ground. Time was everything. They must get across the next stretch of the desert to the track before the alarm was given in the General's camp.

Up the bank and on to the sand again. The cart creaked on for hours. Suddenly there was a shout.

"They've caught us. It's all up," whispered the servant.

Two bearded brigands galloped up to them.

"We saw the marks of your cart," they said, "and it's our business to round up travellers and deserters. Where are you going?"

"To Turkestan," answered the ladies.

"Have you a special permit?"

In a flash Mildred thought of their government passport which every missionary in China carries. She brought it out with all its impressive-looking seals and put it under the noses of the riders. Neither of them could read, but the look of the passport was sufficient. It was so grand. It must be official.

"Pass on," they said.

For four days the travellers pressed on to the frontier through the wilderness of the Gobi. Fearful at each rise in the sandy dunes that they would meet more brigands who would finally arrest them, they drove the mules as hard as possible. There was little to eat for man or beast, and often on the desert floor they passed the signs of wolves, pieces of blood-stained uniforms and the scattered bones of men and horses. Even the maximum speed was only three miles an hour.

In one rocky gorge a man suddenly leaped out in front of them and then leaped back again, while the air was filled with a weird incantation which terrified them. A few hours later one of the three walking alone up a little mound to scan the horizon was caught by the wind, which lifted her off her feet and whirled her to the bottom. She was found staggering about, having lost her sense of time and place. The Gobi wind had bitten deeply and stunned her spirit.

When they were finally out of danger Mildred went to see the mules being fed, thankful to them for their hard work across the perilous miles. Standing by them in the inn stable was a donkey, no doubt ill-used by its Moslem owner. It suddenly lashed out at Mildred, knocked her down and kicked her head open so that she lay with a bleeding head-wound in the filth of the stable floor.

Battered and bruised after their journey, the two friends lifted Mildred into the inn and bathed her head. It was a noisy place and their patient needed quiet. Then they remembered a friend back along the road, one who had invited them into his garden to eat mulberries. A messenger was sent down the road asking him to allow them to pitch their tent amongst his trees. So the heavily bandaged Mildred was carried by the jolting cart out of the inn courtyard to the peace of the garden, where on one side was a row of mulberry trees and on the other a wide view of the Gobi they had just crossed.

The news of the accident spread, and cartloads of visitors began to arrive to look at Mildred and the wonderful bandage round her head. A gang of shouting boys stormed round the tent asking for Scriptures, which they intended to burn—a favourite trick of Moslem boys. Mildred lay weary, tired and in danger of fever if the wound failed to heal.

It was then that the gardener was again appealed to, for the sake of the traveller and for the sake of the good name of the Gobi land which in spite of brigands, war-lords, perils of rivers and sands was a friendly courteous place to the three friends.

"These troublesome boys!" he said; "it takes me all my time to keep them in order. Do not think of moving. We like to have you here." Quiet descended on the little camp and Mildred Cable slept soundly in the healing peace of the Gobi, and under the shade of the mulberry tree.

6

CHILDREN OF THE GOBI

"I HAVE no money, but will you give me a gospel in exchange for this?"

The grubby hand of the little girl held out a home-made roll of steamed bread; she flashed her bright eyes on Mildred Cable. It was a look and an appeal that Mildred and her friends could never resist. They loved the children of the Gobi road, their cheerful, round, fat faces, their padded thick little bodies in winter, their willingness to listen and learn. Soon the streets of the Gobi oasis were alive with children running with bread and new laid eggs for "the Teachers", for the word had gone that they were short of food. Their bag of bread was finished, and the only food they could make was from flour mixed with oil, pulled out into long strips, nipped into small chunks, and boiled in water.

The fresh home-made steamed bread was worth a copy of the gospels and the child ran away home with the precious little book, unable to read it herself but hugging it for someone who could.

When the travellers first started going up and down the Gobi road the children heard their parents whisper all sorts of evil stories about them. They would entice them away to remote places in the sandhills; they would gouge out their eyes, and cut out their hearts, and then by their magic put them all back again so that a child under their power would have to follow them everywhere. Who were these mysterious ladies, one in blue, another in grey and another in brown? Where were their husbands, and their homes? The children of the oases and the towns sat and shuddered as their parents talked of these fearsome newcomers.

But the children's curiosity and friendliness triumphed over their fears. In Suchow whenever the ladies went for a walk a gang of laughing, shouting children followed them through the streets. They ran into the garden where the ladies lived, on the pretence of picking up sticks, but really just to have a look at the strange creatures. Whenever there was a singing lesson a large crowd surged outside the window and seemed to love it so much that Mildred suggested a Children's Service.

The large tent was crowded with children every evening, and the incandescent paraffin lantern shone on the eager, happy faces of the Gobi children. From Britain a consignment of tin instruments had been sent out, and the tent was filled with the noise of a children's orchestra—

tambourines, mouth-organs, jingles and pipes—joining in with the baby organ. All the hymns were sung with bangings, clappings, clangings and stamping of feet, and so great was the joyful noise that crowds of grown-ups came to watch.

One little boy walked out of the tent singing at the top of his voice,

Dare to be a Daniel, dare to stand alone,

and ran down the street to an old peanut seller and looked him straight in the face and spoke words that he learned in the tent,

"Did you *know* that there is only *One* God, and *One* Lord Jesus Christ?"

"Why no," said the old man looking with bewildered surprise at the boy.

"Well, it's true," shouted the boy, and ran on singing,

Dare to have a purpose true and dare to make it known!

The children of Suchow proved to be splendid little missionaries for "the Teachers", and to the courtyard where they lived there came many of the Gobi waifs and strays.

One cold morning a little boy of ten was sitting naked outside the door. He had been out all night, and was crying with pain and hunger. He was led into the kitchen for a good breakfast. He had no home, nor parents that he knew of.

"Where is your daddy?" he was asked.

"Dead," was the answer.

"Then I suppose you want me to be your daddy now?" said Dr. Kao, the Chinese pastor in Suchow.

"Yes, please," said the boy.

*   *   *

It was love of children which made the friends look out for them on their journeys. They saw them in the market places, in the homes, selling cooked beans or peanuts or dried melon seeds. Some of them collected baskets of horse manure to heat the fire underneath the *kang*—the family bed which kept everybody warm in winter. In summer the children played about often with little clothing on, but in winter the bitter Gobi winds swept through the towns and villages on the roads and drove them into corners, huddling together to keep warm.

One of these was little Grace, who originally had the name of "Brothers-to-Follow" which her father Mr. Han the mat weaver gave her because he was so hopeful that his next child would be a boy. Mr. Han, like so many men in the Gobi towns, could have been happy and prosperous because his mats were very popular, and the grass he wove them from grew in the desert free of charge. All he had to do was to go and pick it. But Mr. Han was lazy, loved to gamble, and was always short of money.

On one New Year's Day Mr. Han whispered to his wife as they lay at night on the warm *kang* that something must be done about "Brothers-to-Follow". She must bring some money in. There was only one way, and that was to sell the child to a rich home where they were needing a serving-girl.

It was sad news for Mrs. Han and the child. They sat and wept for a whole day, but in the end Mrs. Han said,

"It is no use crying, there is no escape; it is the will of heaven."

So little "Brothers-to-Follow" had her hair combed, her face washed, and was dressed in a flowery coat Mr. Han managed to borrow for the occasion and was taken off to be sold. It was exciting at first going from house to house, but no one wanted her. She had a big flat nose and big sprawling feet and was so small that people said she could never carry anything.

At last a bargain was struck between her father and a mistress who wanted a child in her house to wait on her. It was a hard, dull life in that house with a mistress who always had a whip handy to punish her. If she was clumsy in waiting she was made to stand with a brick on her head. If it fell she had a cut from the whip. For food she had to pick up the scraps from the kitchen. In the long cold winter there was no warm *kang* for little "Brothers-to-Follow", although she had to keep the *kang* of her master and mistress always warm.

One night it was so cold that she fell asleep on the frozen ground without covering, and the chilblains on her feet turned into black sores so that her foot became dead and useless. She crouched in a corner, miserable, lonely and ill. There she was seen by a visitor to the house.

"She has a bad foot," said Mr. Fu her master; "she can't even serve tea. She's useless."

"I have a doctor friend in the city," said the visitor, "who will cure her."

"She's not worth curing," replied Mr. Fu. His wife was angry that anyone should notice "Brothers-to-Follow" and when the visitor was gone the child was beaten. But the visitor came again, and suggested to Mr. Fu that if he did not allow the child to be treated the public would hear about it.

"Let them have the wretched little thing," screamed Mrs. Fu. So "Brothers-to-Follow" was carried away to the house of the three ladies, and found herself in a warm bed. Before long the frostbitten foot had been attended to, and the child, christened Grace, was adopted into the ladies' home.

* * *

There she met Little Lonely, another adopted waif of the Gobi road. Grace was a cripple, but Little Lonely was deaf as well as dumb, and she came tap, tapping to the ladies' door begging for something to eat. As she could not tell her story, but only smile at the ladies with her dark, solemn eyes, they had to discover her story bit by bit.

Born away in the Tibetan hills Little Lonely, or Topsy as she was called by the ladies, was unwanted by her mother, so a foster mother was found for her who loved the pretty little baby with the satin cap and the silver bells dangling from each side. But when Little Lonely turned out to be dumb she lost her love and turned her away into the streets to beg.

Out on the streets Little Lonely was not a very good beggar, and her foster mother beat her so cruelly for bringing home so little that her legs were marked with bruises. The dogs too bit her legs when she called at the big houses. Her thin, ragged dress was pierced by the cruel winter winds, and her cough was so bad that she could hardly drag herself about the streets. Only a very few coppers did Little Lonely collect, and because they were so few her foster mother hated her.

One day she came back wearing a lovely pair of new trousers which the ladies had made for her, a few copper coins, three little lumps of coal, and a bone which the cook in a food-shop had thrown to her. When Little Lonely fell asleep that night her foster mother pulled the trousers off her legs, leaving her with her old ragged ones, and hurried down to an old clothes shop where the precious trousers were exchanged for a few coppers which bought a lump of opium.

It was the saddest morning in Little Lonely's sad life to wake up without the trousers her ladies had given to her. But that event helped to bring about the big change in Little Lonely's life, for soon the foster mother agreed to allow Little Lonely to live with the ladies always, and the woman's eyes glistened when she saw the money given to her.

With her black hair well combed and plaited into two pig-tails, Topsy grew into a big smiling girl. Her high cheek bones showed her Mongolian ancestry and so did her wilful ways. One day when visitors came to tea Topsy was greedy about the tempting sweetmeats laid out on the table. Some of them mysteriously disappeared, but Topsy shook her head when asked whether she knew where they were. Topsy wore a pair of trousers that day very wide at the ankles, and as she stood to greet the visitors the sweets came rattling down inside the trousers. She had stuffed them inside and forgot there was nothing to hold them from falling to the ground. Topsy had to stand in a corner that afternoon in disgrace for not telling the truth.

As she could not speak or hear, Topsy could not go to school like Grace her friend. It was a great day when Grace, dressed in her finest clothes, with a big bundle of books and belongings, went away down the road towards China to go to school. There Grace grew into a handsome girl of eighteen and, although she was a cripple, Samuel, one of the Chinese young men of the mission, fell in love with her and the ladies were glad to give their permission for Grace to be married.

But Topsy they took with them over the Gobi. Topsy loved riding the cart, but she loved camels best of all. When the camel knelt for Topsy to get on it she gripped the tuft of hair on its hump very firmly, and held on tightly as the camel gradually stretched its long legs and stood with Topsy high and smiling on its back. She quickly got used to the rolling motion of the camel as the beast swung to and fro across the sandy track, for, after all, Topsy was a daughter of the open air, a child of the plains and the mountains.

The camel men liked to see her, for they recognized her as one of themselves although she could not speak. One day a fearful red glow spread over the Gobi sky as Topsy and her ladies trekked northwards to Urumchi.

"Sandstorm coming!" shouted the men.

Suddenly the sands were caught by a tearing whirlwind, and Topsy clung to her camel's hump for fear of being blown off. When the storm gathered force the driver shouted a word of command and the beasts all knelt, stretched out their necks and buried their noses in the sand. Topsy slipped over her hump and knelt behind the camel, hiding her face in its soft hair while the wind blew over them.

Topsy loved pictures, and when they were back in the garden-home at Suchow her favourite was one of Princess Elizabeth, now Queen Elizabeth. The picture of the Princess with golden hair, blue eyes and a dress with flowers on it fascinated the little Mongolian. It was pinned on the wall by Topsy's bed and in her mute language she would ask the ladies about the Princess.

"Is she always good?"

"Can she read and write?"

"Does she spin as I do?"

"Does she always do as she is told?"

"Does she say grace before she eats?"

"Can she knit?"

When Topsy was naughty the worst punishment was to turn the picture of Princess Elizabeth to the wall. How strange it was, the ladies thought, that

6

a little child thousands of miles away should so influence the Mongolian waif who could not hear or speak.

Although Topsy was so handicapped she had other ways of speaking and hearing. Her sharp eyes never missed anything. Through her face and eyes Topsy spoke very intelligently, and she learned to watch other people's faces and eyes. All through the country of the brigands and the bandits she watched the ladies' faces. When a man on horseback rode up, their faces went white. Then the Blue Lady would unfold a big sheet of paper covered with a lot of marks, and smiles came again over all the faces.

Topsy always thought the desert a clean place but she saw dead horses lying about, bones which had been picked over by the wolves, and scraps of soldiers' uniforms. Farther and farther away from her home the cart and the camels took Topsy, until they came at last to Urumchi. Could they take Topsy any further? Could they take her to Britain? The ladies had many anxious talks about this because Topsy had no passport; in fact, she had no name.

For Mildred Cable it was a hard and heavy problem, for Topsy was probably dearer to her than anyone else. The little waif had captured her heart. Her own Chinese name was *Gai*, so Topsy was given the surname of *Guy*. Topsy's own first name was *Ai Lien* so her Christian name became *Eileen*.

Equipped with this information Mildred Cable set out to get permission for Eileen Guy to cross the frontier into Russia. The British Consul did his best, but the most formidable obstacle was a stern lady in a building bearing the sign of the hammer and sickle. Every few days Mildred and Topsy went to see her but every day the answer was "No". Topsy soon knew how "No" looked on the lady's face. Then one day it was "Yes" with a smile, and Topsy wept tears of joy. The stern lady too jumped up and took Topsy in her arms and kissed her.

7

THE TRAIL LEADS ON

CITY of Seagulls! Perched high in a Russian peasant cart the trio and Topsy came to the borders of Russia. Piotr their driver jingled his horses along, flourishing a short-handled whip, urging them on to the City of Seagulls, or Chuguchak, where they might cross into the great unknown land of Siberia. It was a bumpy, lively three weeks in the cart to the City of Seagulls with the trail leading on across the wide, tilled acres of Turkestan where the grain, the apples, the pears and grapes were being harvested.

It was harvest time, too, in Mildred's heart as she sat there in the cart, or watched the kettle boil by the streams they stopped at to drink tea. In the tea they soaked their dry bread, and under the open sky of Turkestan Mildred thought of the future.

Five times she and her friends had been up and down this road distributing the Scriptures, talking with the people, visiting the bazaars and making friends for Christ's sake. "Here's the gospel back again, back again, back again" was the refrain in the market towns and amongst the inn-keepers.

The years had been hard but glorious. She would start all over again, but she also knew that all over those vast, lonely miles on the roof of the world a new day was dawning in brigandage and revolt. Communism was creeping along the trails of the Gobi, and the might of Russia was making itself felt along the trade routes she had known so well.

On to the City of Seagulls rattled the cart, with Piotr eager to show his travellers how well he could drive them into the streets of the city. But Mildred's alert eye had caught sight of a camp of the Kazak people, sturdy people always on the move, tent-dwellers but highly intelligent. A handsome young woman in an olive green dress and riding breeches and with a pink kerchief on her head came out to meet them. Her tent was covered with heavy rugs, and big metal faced boxes held her clothes and all her household goods. She had a brother away in Moscow learning the new ways of Communism and the Soviet Union, and she herself was aware of many happenings in the big, wide world she had never seen. As they left her standing at her tent door Mildred thought of the many splendid people she was leaving behind in the world of the Gobi—a world which was changing and which needed Christ all the more.

It was Saturday afternoon in the City of Seagulls. Topsy was excited to see the women at their wash-tubs washing their cotton dresses to wear on Sunday, for in this city the Russian Orthodox Church had one of its churches. When Mildred woke up she could tell it was Sunday, for there was a "Sunday atmosphere" so different from the pagan unconcern she had been used to.

The little church was crowded with people, and in the afternoon the trio went to another service where the worship was just a simple testimony to the power of the Bible. These two experiences made Mildred think all the more of the harvest which might yet be gathered in these lonely out-posts.

But the trail led on across the border into Russia, and this time the cart was a Russian tarantass which Mildred described as rather like "a large tea-tray laid on four wheels". The trio and Topsy sat on its edge, dangling their legs, with their luggage piled in the middle. They had four rugs, four pillows, two large bags of sun-dried crusts and one pot of jam, a bag of *zamba* (a kind of cornflour which made a quick and nourishing gruel with hot water) and a few bricks of tea—compressed into solid lumps from the leavings of the tea-shops. They had no money, as Russia prohibited taking money over the border.

*   *   *

As the tarantass rocked across the border between China and Russia the trio knew that they were leaving behind their old world and facing a new start. At the Chinese frontier, when their baggage had been examined and their passports stamped, they gathered in a little group with their Chinese friends and as a farewell salute to China sang their journeying hymn:

> *Guide me, O Thou great Jehovah,*
> *Pilgrim through this barren land;*
>
> *Let the fiery cloudy pillar*
> *Guide me all my journey through.*

There were tears in many eyes as they turned towards Baxti where the motor postal van would take them to the railhead. For Topsy it meant leaving behind her homeland and trusting entirely in the "Mamas" who had taken her to their hearts. For Mildred Cable it was the final break in thirty-six years of service in China.

From a Gobi cart, a Russian cart, and a tarantass, to a huge heavy lorry which pounded down the road to Sergiopol for seventeen hours all through the night. There were no seats in this bus, and at the wayside stops luggage, mail and boxes of goods were thrown in anyhow. At midnight a crowd of young men leaped out of the darkness with a consignment of heavy boxes, bales and steel girders.

A huge, naked saw was thrown across Mildred so that she was in danger as the lorry lurched forward of being impaled on its sharp teeth. The lorry itself, so loaded and laden, refused to move, and the driver shouted, "Comrades! my engine will not carry this load. Comrades! my engine will not work." That did the trick. The same hands which threw the burdens on to the lorry threw them off again, and into the darkness of the unknown road the trio, with Topsy snuggled close to them on the floor of the truck, rattled further on into Russia.

From Sergiopol to Moscow the train rumbled on day after day going westwards, nearing home. On the crowded wooden seats of the compartment Mildred, with a Russian phrase book, managed to keep a conversation going. When an inspector questioned a detail on the trio's tickets, and would have seized their baggage and thrown it out of the train, the whole compartment rose up in anger to stop him. At every station the travellers rushed to the hot water taps on the platform to make their tea, and every time some young man sprang forward to help them. Wide eyed, Topsy followed every moment of the long journey with excited interest, and stared with fascination at the big station in Moscow where they had to sleep in the station dormitory provided for travellers unable to get into a hotel. Topsy stared even more when they got to Berlin, where there were clean white sheets in a bed, and a whole hot bath to herself.

But when they got to London on an autumn day in 1938 Topsy had reached the limit of wondering, for this was the home of her "Mamas" and now this was home for her. She loved the big red London buses, and the friendly people who came by them to the meetings the trio spoke at, but they were all happiest in the little cottage in the west country where there was space and quiet.

*   *   *

It was there in the country where she could see the stars, and think about the stars shining clear over the Gobi Desert, that Mildred Cable began to plan her future life. But for Mildred to plan was to wait, and to expect that God would show her ways in which the trail of life would still lead on in His service. She was not disappointed.

One day, as the ominous news of the second world war invaded the quiet of the countryside, a visitor came to the cottage. He was the bearer of a message. Would Mildred throw her energies and her gifts into the work of the British and Foreign Bible Society? Again for Mildred Cable "something happened" and for the next fourteen years she journeyed about Britain telling the wonderful story of how the Bible came, how it is translated and distributed to-day. She looked upon this task as a continuation of her trail across the Gobi—there she sowed the seed, and now she helped to provide the resources for other sowers out on the trails of the distant continents and islands. For all Mildred Cable's life was part of the same pattern—following the star of God's guidance wherever it led.

With the war over, the opportunity came to spread her wings again over the seas, and this time to Australia, New Zealand and India. There she was fascinated not so much by the big cities as by the wild, unvisited parts. From the window of the overland train she watched the endless vistas of the Australian Desert and thought of her own Gobi. She was interested to see that even in the saltbush flat lands sheep-farming was possible, and that wherever the gum tree flourished there was always enough wood to make a good fire—so unlike the slow, smoky fires she had been used to in the Gobi. She was fascinated, too, by the "Abos" of Australia, the Aborigines who live in the bush and love above all to wander or to "walk-about" as they call it. She noticed the difference between those who had come into contact with Christian missions and those who still remained degraded and wretched, begging for a coin from passing travellers. She met a great crowd of Abo children who came up to the train to greet her. "They were so happy," she wrote, "so full of life, so suitably dressed and they sang to us the hymns that our own children sing. When at last the train was about to move out of the station the passengers said to each other, 'Look at those children. They say that nothing can be done with an Abo, but look at them!' " Mildred Cable thought of the long years trekking across the Gobi and seeing something of the wonders that God creates in human lives, and she said quietly to herself, "With men it is impossible, but not with God."

Her heart was stirred again as she stood in the holy city of Benares in India and watched the thousands of pilgrims dipping themselves in the River Ganges. The water's edge was crowded with men and women performing their rites of bowing towards the sun, and then stepping down into the river and letting the sacred water cover them, and not forgetting to drink a little of it. As they stepped out of the water a priest was ready to apply the caste marks to each one as the crowds moved back into the dark temples to make their obeisance to the gods.

Mildred's heart was revolted by the scenes of idolatry, filth and superstition which she saw in the streets, with the faces of evil men predominating amongst the great crowds. Here and there she saw a refined face, a modest pilgrim, a humble-looking man making his way to the sacred river, and she longed to be able to preach to them in their own language as she was able to do along the trails of the Gobi.

Most unexpectedly the same day she slipped back again amongst the people she had once known. She was taken to visit a Buddhist Abbot living in his bare, simple temple just as if he was on the side of the road in Gobi-land. In his yellow robe he graciously opened his guest-room to his visitor and was delighted when Mildred spoke to him in Chinese. Bowls of tea were brought and slowly sipped, holding the bowl with both hands. The Buddhists were there in Benares to try to revive the Buddhist faith in India's sacred city, and Mildred saluted in them fellow-missionaries, each eager to spread his own religion. She sent him a Bible in Chinese as a token of her respect and her hope that the Good News might reach his heart.

*　　*　　*

But Mildred could never remain long away from the frontier posts of the faith, so she eagerly accepted an invitation to the mountains of Assam for a Bible Sunday amongst the Khasi people, with children carrying faggots of wood for the collection. Not many years before her visit the tribes were scalping one another and burying the scalps with a dead chief in his grave, believing he would need those men as his servants in the next world. When a travelling missionary visited them the chief presented him with a two-edged scalping sword, saying, "With this sword we once killed men, but now we have no more use for it, for our desire is to win men to Christ." To hear stories such as this on the hills of Assam was again an assurance to Mildred Cable that the Bibles she had distributed along the trails of the Gobi might even then be bearing fruit, and that out of her own life-service miracles might yet be recorded.

Another frontier quest led her northwards to the country which borders the world she had known along the Gobi with India. Although separated from it by long mountainous chains, the feeling of going northward lifted Mildred Cable's heart at Amritsar. There she saw the beautiful temple of the Sikhs, the Golden Temple, where no one wears ordinary shoes and most visitors go in barefooted. The sacred tank of water is over five hundred feet long, with many bathers constantly using it. There, too, the sacred Sikh volume, the *Granth*, rests and is carried in every morning to the shrine and out every evening to its separate lodging place. Only special people called *granthi* may read the book, and a relay of them take turns to wave a yak's tail over it lest a fly or an insect should alight on the sacred book.

* * *

It was memories of scenes like this which

spurred Mildred Cable on to even greater efforts for the Bible Society when she returned to Britain. The Bible for her was a book for all men to read in their own language, and her spirit would never rest until she had given all she could in the cause of spreading the Scriptures. She was in regular demand as a speaker at great meetings, and wherever her name was announced large audiences came to be inspired by her experiences both on the Gobi and from her later journeys. In 1951 she and Francesca French set out again on another trail leading them southwards, this time to South America, ranging through the cities but always delighting in discovering the remote places and hearing of faithful work done in loneliness. Mildred Cable's mind was always seeking to understand what Christ was saying to the "regions beyond", and she was always ready to walk down the trails which had never been trodden before.

But 1952 found her very tired. As part of the preparation for the Third Jubilee of the Bible Society she had written a popular story of the society called *Why not for the World?* It was her last gift to the work she loved, for on the last day of April 1952, as spring was beginning to spread over the land, she died.

But although Mildred Cable is no longer to be seen walking the earth, preparing for some long journey, or planning once again to cross the Gobi

Desert, she is still on the trail for Christ. Her memory inspires others, and the news of her adventures in His name are part of the Christian history which she helped to make.

For her friends who shared her life—Evangeline and Francesca French—there is the memory of a noble work which cannot die, and for Topsy, now a grown woman, and quite used to the ways of London and the friendly interest of its people, there is the loving remembrance of "the blue gowned Mama" who took a waif from the Gobi and loved it into new life. And the great company of noble pioneers for Christ makes room for Mildred Cable who on the last page of the last book she wrote says, "Without God we cannot: without us, God will not."

This story of Mildred Cable is based chiefly on the following books written either by herself, or in collaboration with Francesca French:

THROUGH JADE GATE
A DESERT JOURNAL
THE GOBI DESERT
SOMETHING HAPPENED
THE STORY OF TOPSY
JOURNEY WITH A PURPOSE

All published by Hodder and Stoughton Ltd.

WALL OF SPEARS (*Lutterworth*)